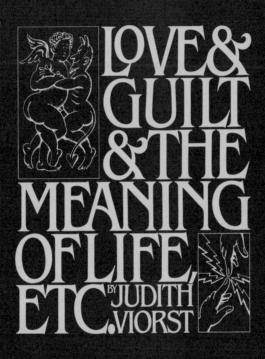

LOVE & GUILT & THE MEANING OF LIFE, ETC. BY JUDITH VIORST

Books by Judith Viorst

A Visit From St. Nicholas
to a Liberated Household

How Did I Get to Be Forty and Other Atrocities

The Village Square

Sunday Morning

It's Hard to Be Hip Over Thirty and
Other Tragedies of Married Life

I'll Fix Anthony

Try It Again, Sam

People and Other Aggravations

The Tenth Good Thing About Barney

Yes, Married

Alexander and the Terrible, Horrible,
No Good, Very Bad Day

My Mama Says There Aren't Any Zombies,
Ghosts, Vampires, Creatures, Demons, Monsters,
Fiends, Goblins or Things

Rosie and Michael

Alexander, Who Used to Be Rich Last Sunday

Illustrations by John Alcorn
Design by Herb Lubalin

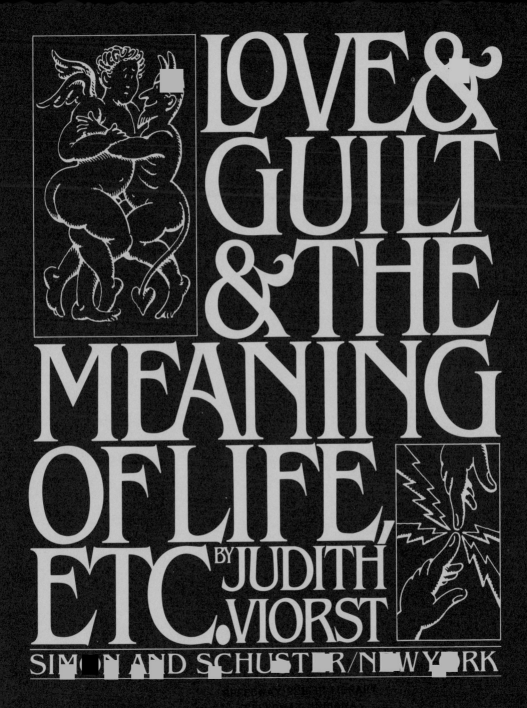

LOVE & GUILT & THE MEANING OF LIFE, ETC.

BY JUDITH VIORST

SIMON AND SCHUSTER/NEW YORK

Published by Simon and Schuster
A Division of Gulf & Western Corporation
Simon & Schuster Building
Rockefeller Center
1230 Avenue of the Americas
New York, New York 10020

Much of the material in this book
first appeared, in somewhat different
form, in *Redbook* magazine.

Designed by Herb Lubalin and Michael Aron
Illustrations by John Alcorn

Manufactured in the United States of America

1   2   3   4   5   6   7   8   9   10

Library of Congress Cataloging
in Publication Data

Viorst, Judith.
      Love and guilt and the meaning of life, etc.

      I. Title.
PS3572.I6L6   818'.5'402   78-27299

ISBN 0-671-22869-2

FOR MY
SISTER
LOIS

LOVE: Love is agreeing with him completely when he needs you to agree with him completely, and telling him the plain unvarnished truth when he needs you to tell him the plain unvarnished truth, and knowing when he needs which.

LOVE AND INFATUATION:
Infatuation is when you think that he's as gorgeous as Robert Redford, as pure as Solzhenitsyn, as funny as Woody Allen, as athletic as Jimmy Connors, and as smart as Albert Einstein. Love is when you realize that he's as gorgeous as Woody Allen, as smart as Jimmy Connors, as funny as Solzhenitsyn, as athletic as Albert Einstein, and nothing like Robert Redford in any category—but you'll take him anyway.

THE END OF LOVE:
It seems to me that when a man informs a woman he loved that he no longer loves her, she has two choices: She can weep and carry on and fall apart. Or she can recall their beautiful moments together and feel very grateful and thankful for what they had—and then weep and carry on and fall apart.

LOVE AND LUST:
Lust is what makes you keep wanting to do it, even when you have no desire to be with each other. Love is what makes you keep wanting to be with each other, even when you have no desire to do it.

LOVE AND CRITICISM
(I): Just because you tell someone that he's cold, cruel, insensitive, stingy, lacking in human decency, and balding doesn't always mean that you don't love him.

LOVE AND CRITICISM
(II): Just because you tell someone that he's cold, cruel, insensitive, stingy, lacking in human decency, and balding doesn't always mean that you don't hate him, either.

STAR-CROSSED LOVE:
The closest my husband and I ever get to being star-crossed lovers is when he thinks he's meeting me by the frozen-vegetable counter, and I think he's meeting me by the sour cream.

6

WHAT IS
THIS THING
CALLED LOVE:
Love is what makes a person who is philosophically opposed to monogamous sexual relationships on the grounds that jealousy and possessiveness between women and men are not intrinsic to human nature but simply the out-moded by-products of a decadent capitalistic system, take it all back.

NEUROTIC
LOVE:
According to my friend Stanley the Psychiatrist, neurotic love is when, if you play hard to get, he thinks that you're rejecting him. And when, if you play easy to get, he thinks that you're absurdly undiscriminating. And when, if you play just right to get, neither too hard nor too easy, he thinks that you're controlling and manipulative. And when, if he still decides that he wants to marry you, you accept.

LOVE
AND
SECURITY:
Have you noticed that when you deeply love a man and he deeply loves you, and you feel completely secure in each other's love, you don't have to laugh at his jokes unless they're funny?

FALLING IN LOVE:

In my day, when a girl fell in love, her mother ardently hoped it would be with a boy of the same race, color, and creed. But nowadays, when a girl falls in love, her mother only hopes it will be with a boy.

BEING IN LOVE:

Being in love is better than being in jail, a dentist's chair, or a holding pattern over Philadelphia, but not if he doesn't love you back.

PROOF OF LOVE:

There were just three things, a now-divorced lady told me, that her former husband thought she ought to do to prove to him she really truly loved him: One, make fresh orange juice for breakfast. Two, check his shirts for missing buttons. And three, give up thinking that foreplay was necessary.

LOVE TALK:

Brevity may be the soul of wit, but not when someone's saying "I love you." When someone's saying "I love you," he always ought to give a lot of details: Like, Why does he love you? And, How much does he love you? And, When and where did he first begin to love you? Favorable comparisons with all the other women he ever loved are also welcome. And even though he insists it would take forever to count the ways in which he loves you, let him start counting.

HUSBANDLY
LOVE: When a husband says that he loves you so much that he thinks about you morning, noon, and night, chances are that he's somebody else's husband.

WIFELY
LOVE: When a woman says that she'd rather sleep with her husband than Warren Beatty, chances are that Warren never asked her.

WHAT IS
THIS THING
CALLED LOVE: Love is when it's 10 P.M., and you get this gnawing need for fudge-brownie ice cream, and even though you're not even sick or pregnant, he drives to Baskin-Robbins and buys you some. Note: If he goes around telling people about it at parties, deduct twenty points from his score.

LOVE
AND
MARRIAGE: One advantage of marriage, it seems to me, is that when you fall out of love with him, or he falls out of love with you, it keeps you together until you maybe fall in again.

MORE LOVE
AND
SECURITY: Have you noticed that when you deeply love a man and he deeply loves you, and you feel completely secure in each other's love, he always lets you know when your hair looks awful?

LOVING AND LOSING:

According to my friend Doris the Dieter, it is better to have loved and lost than it is to have loved and put on fifteen pounds.

A QUESTION OF LOVE:

When someone asks your husband to describe the relationship between love and marriage, is it nice for him to answer, "What relationship?"

LOVE AND SHRIMP:

The courtship: He offers you the last shrimp in his shrimp cocktail and you say, "No, thank you."

The engagement: He offers you the last shrimp in his shrimp cocktail and you accept it.

The beginning of the marriage: He no longer offers you the last shrimp in his shrimp cocktail but, whenever you ask for it, he gives it to you.

Later in the marriage: He not only no longer offers you the last shrimp in his shrimp cocktail but, whenever you ask for it, he says he wishes you'd order your own shrimp cocktail.

Still later in the marriage: He not only no longer offers you the last shrimp in his shrimp cocktail but, if he ever offered, you wouldn't accept it.

The end of the marriage: You decide that shrimp is a metaphor for love.

WHAT IS THIS THING CALLED LOVE:
Love is when you and he take a shower together, and you finish first, and one towel is soggy and damp, and one towel is dry, and you use the soggy and damp towel and leave him the dry one. Note: Deduct twenty points from your score if you tell him you did it.

LESSON IN LOVE:
If he doesn't love you because you can't learn to recognize inept translations from the Greek, or tell real French Provincial from the fake, or know when a concert pianist is playing the lentamente part too lento, or understand when a pas de deux is superior and when it's merely adequate, he will not love you even if you learn to.

LOVE TEST:
Question: How do you distinguish love from like?

Answer: Love is the same as like except you feel sexier. And more romantic. And also more annoyed when he talks with his mouth full. And you also resent it more when he interrupts you. And you also respect him less when he shows any weakness. Furthermore, when you ask if he'll come to pick you up at the airport, and he tells you that he can't because he's busy, it's only when you love him that you hate him.

GUILT: Although it is sometimes better to sin and feel guilty than never to sin at all, it is pretty ratty to sin and not feel guilty. Things to feel guilty about should include leaving toenail clippings in the ashtray, hanging up the phone instead of saying "Sorry, I must have dialed the wrong number," and being nicer to people who are terrible but famous than you are to people who are just plain terrible.

SPIRITUAL GUILT: Praying, instead of for peace on earth, that your hair will look terrific tomorrow morning.

HOW TO GET OUT OF ADMITTING YOU'RE GUILTY EVEN THOUGH YOU'RE GUILTY: Deny it. Accuse <u>him</u> of doing it. Tell him he drove you to it. Tell him it doesn't count because you hated it.

GUILTLESSNESS, OR VISITING THE FATHER'S SINS UPON THE CHILD: Coming home from a cocktail party at which your husband has flirted all night with the hostess, and smacking your kid for messing up the living room.

GUILTY OR INNOCENT TEST

(BEGINNERS): Do you ever serve something fattening to someone on a diet and swear to her that it only has twenty calories?

Do you ever buy someone a present at your local discount store and put it in a Saks Fifth Avenue box?

Do you ever let someone who thinks you come from Boston instead of Brooklyn keep on thinking it?

And you don't call that sneaky?

GUILT AND THE SINGLE GIRL:

Finding it harder to say no to a fellow after an evening of filet mignon and champagne than it is to say no to a fellow after a cheeseburger.

GUILT AND FORGIVENESS:

Always do your best to get a promise of forgiveness before you actually make an admission of guilt. Say, "How can I possibly tell you, you'd never forgive me." Say, "Even you aren't wise and mature and sensitive enough to forgive me for this." Say you want it in writing.

COMPLEX
GUILT: My friend Louise feels guilty, she says, whenever she takes a taxi instead of giving the money to the Heart Fund. Furthermore, she feels guilty, she says, about wanting to be admired for feeling guilty.

NO-FAULT
GUILT: This is when, instead of trying to figure out who's to blame, everyone pays.

LIVING
WITH
GUILT: Under certain circumstances, says Dotty who just got divorced, confession may be better for the soul than it is for the marriage.

GUILTY OR
INNOCENT TEST
(INTERMEDIATE): Are you the kind of person who would never pet a dog if you and the dog were the only ones in the room?

Would you pick up the cans that you knocked off the shelf at the Safeway if you were alone in the aisle when you knocked them down?

Does the presence of an audience determine whether you say to your child, "No, no, no, my darling, mustn't do that," instead of, "Cut that out or I'll smash you one"?

Or do you always assume that you're being spied on?

GUILT IS RELATIVE:
A serious dieter is a woman who, having dined sumptuously at an Italian restaurant with a married man and then gone to bed with him, feels guiltier about the former than the latter.

BAD-MOTHER GUILT:
It is all right to leave your sick child with a sitter to go to a PTA meeting or to a save-the-whale meeting or to the drugstore to buy a heating pad. It is not all right to leave your sick child to go to a movie or out to lunch with friends or to the drugstore to buy eyeliner.

BAD-DAUGHTER GUILT:
My friend Arlene feels guilty because she only calls her mother once a month but her mother never reproaches her or complains. She says that she wishes her mother would start reproaching her and complaining so instead of guilty she could feel resentful.

EXERCISE GUILT:
Claiming that you do thirty sit-ups a day, when you really do thirty sit-ups a day twice a week.

GUILTY OR INNOCENT TEST

(ADVANCED): Do you, when you go to pay by check, expect to be suspected of not being you?

Do you, in the process of paying by check, even start thinking that maybe you <u>aren't</u> you?

Do you therefore try to pretend to the person you're paying by check that you really <u>are</u> you?

Or is it just me who's crazy?

INTELLECTUAL GUILT:

Looking as if you are sunk in deep thought when what you are actually thinking is whether your coral lipstick goes with your sweater.

GUILT AND THE VISITING MOTHER:

Sunday: How long has he been walking around with that cough?

Monday: <u>This</u> you call a nourishing breakfast for children?

Tuesday: I wouldn't ask you to close that window but maybe you could lend me a couple of sweaters.

Wednesday: If you really want to go out for an hour and leave me here in the house by myself alone, it's up to you.

Thursday: Your brother has always been such a thoughtful son.

Friday: I'll take the bus to the airport so you won't have to interrupt your phone conversation.

MILT
GUILT: This is the guilt that I feel about things that I'd never feel guilty about if Milton my husband didn't tell me I ought to. Like, liking canned asparagus better than fresh ones. And not knowing state capitals. And throwing out an unused stamp instead of trying to peel it off the envelope.

QUILT
GUILT: Always hogging more than your share of the covers.

WILT
GUILT: When you didn't water a house plant that, if only you had watered it, wouldn't have died.

BUILT
GUILT: Wishing flab, cellulite, sagging breasts, and a weight gain of forty pounds upon a woman of whom your husband approvingly says, "Boy, she's really built."

GUILT
GUILT: Morty my cousin feels guilty, he says, about not feeling guilty. He wants to know if that counts.

GUILTY OR INNOCENT TEST (GRADUATE STUDENTS ONLY):

When your kid drops a truck on your toe and you're not wearing shoes, and your car gets a flat in the rain and you just had your hair done, and, as you walk up the steps to your house, the bottom falls out of the grocery bag with the eggs, do you think you're being punished for something you did?

Furthermore, do you think you <u>deserve</u> to be punished?

Even if you don't know what you did?

BENEFITS OF GUILT:

Guilt keeps you from doing rotten mean awful things that would hurt other people. Guilt keeps you from doing wonderful marvelous things that wouldn't hurt anyone else but are bad for your character. Guilt lets you do lots of wonderful marvelous things that wouldn't hurt anyone else but are bad for your character because, by feeling guilty, you prove that your character really isn't so bad.

THE
MEANING OF
LIFE: Along with the police emergency number,
a good recipe for quiche, and a hairdresser who'll
always work you in, the meaning of life is also a nice
thing to know.

HAPPINESS: Who needs it? Show me a happy
person and I'll show you a very worried human
being, a human being who is always asking, What
did I ever do to deserve such happiness? And,
What and how much am I going to have to pay for
it? And, When will it be discovered that this
happiness was not intended for me but for the
lady next door?

DEATH: I'm still hoping someone will make me
a better offer.

TRUTH: Ye shall know the truth and ye shall
hate it. In other words, if you insist upon knowing
whether your husband is sleeping with Marjorie
Cooper, don't expect to be crazy about the answer.

SEX: The same kind of women who used to insist
they were virgins now go around insisting that
they're insatiable, and we're still lying about sex as
much as ever.

SUFFERING: Suffering makes you deep. Travel makes you broad. In case I get my pick, I'd rather travel.

INNER SERENITY: My friend Amy says that when the world is falling to pieces all around you, and you nevertheless feel inwardly serene, it probably means that your hair is looking good.

FRIENDSHIP: A friend is someone who tells you you need a breath freshener. And that your skirt makes funny bulges across your behind. And that the veal in your veal Marsala is dry and stringy. And that Marjorie Cooper is meeting your husband for lunch. And I think I need something friendlier than friendship.

COURAGE: When you go ahead and do something even though you're so utterly terrified of doing it that you're crying and shaking and fainting and throwing up, that is called courage. Or is it called stupidity?

WISDOM: Wisdom is the ability to distinguish between courage and stupidity.

COMPLAINING (EVERYTHING YOU ALWAYS WANTED TO KNOW ABOUT IT): Question: What is the basic purpose of complaining?

Answer: To get help. To get sympathy. To get admiration. Or to make the person who's being complained to feel guilty and ashamed, plus rotten, depressed, depraved, and sick at heart.

Question: How should a person who's being complained to give help?

Answer: By making what's being complained about go away, which it won't by saying, "I told you so," or, "You should have talked to Uncle Bernie's lawyer."

Question: What should you wear when complaining?

Answer: Sportswear by day. Something a little dressier at night. Anything, as long as it doesn't make your listener say, "No wonder you say you're freezing—look what you're wearing."

Question: What is the preferred method of complaint?

Answer: The whine. According to a recent national poll, 42 per cent prefer whining, followed by nagging (28 per cent), recrimination (17 per cent), and other.

Question: What is the rudest thing you can do while complaining?

Answer: There are many rude things you can do while complaining, like complaining with your mouth full or complaining while you're standing on someone's foot, but the rudest thing of all is complaint one-upmanship. This entails having a higher fever, a worse marriage, greater debts, and a more deprived childhood than anyone who complains to you.

DEPRESSION: I have always admired people who get depressed only over high-minded things like famines in Africa and the plight of the Indian, and who never get depressed over low-minded things like the dryer is broken. And I'll never be one.

**THE
GOLDEN
MEAN:** This is an indeterminate point lying somewhere between If at first you don't succeed, try, try again, and Enough is enough.

CLEAN: Certain questions return again and again to trouble the soul. Like, suppose you're stirring the soup and you taste the soup with the spoon with which you've been stirring and then you stick the spoon back in the soup without washing it. Would you still be entitled to call yourself a clean person?

JUSTICE: Justice is when he chooses an incredibly homely woman with a profoundly beautiful soul over an incredibly beautiful woman with a profoundly shallow soul. There is no justice.

GROWING
OLD: I'd rather grow azaleas.

WINNING: It isn't important. What really counts is how you play the game.

LOSING: It isn't important. What really counts is how you play the game.

PLAYING
THE
GAME: Play to win.

SELF-
CONFIDENCE: When you think that your greatest fault is being too hard on yourself.

SUPERSTITION: Superstition is foolish, childish, primitive, and irrational, but how much does it cost you to knock on wood?

COMPASSION: If people do harm to you and you do not get angry with them, but instead make an effort to understand the unconscious fears and unresolved hostilities that prompted them to act in such a fashion, you're bound to develop compassion. Or maybe a skin rash.

COMPLAINING:
(SOME MORE THINGS YOU WANTED
TO KNOW ABOUT IT): Question: Is
complaining good for your teeth?

Answer: Yes. It is hard to complain and grind your teeth simultaneously.

Question: Does complaining get rid of split ends?

Answer: Only if, in the course of complaining, you tear out your hair.

Question: Can complaining help your sex life?

Answer: Yes, if what you're complaining about is that he's such a wonderful lover that you can't ever get enough of his glorious body. No, if what you're complaining about is that George, whom you almost married, did it better.

Question: What are some of the common complaints about love?

Answer: He doesn't love me. He doesn't love me enough. He doesn't love me for the right things (i.e., my soul as distinct from my body). He doesn't love me the way I want to be loved (i.e., the way that Heathcliff loved Cathy). He doesn't love me as much as he loves his mother, his dog, his job, his MG, his Sunday morning tennis game, or his wife.

BEAUTY: I find it difficult to reconcile the concept that beauty is truth and truth beauty with orthodontia and nose bobs.

STRENGTH: Strength is the capacity to break a Hershey bar into four pieces with your own bare hands—and then to eat just one of the pieces.

MEMORY: As I've already mentioned, certain questions return again and again to trouble the soul. Like, how come a person who can't remember Hamlet's soliloquy, or Gresham's law, or the date of the Spanish Armada, or the subjunctive of <u>pouvoir</u>, can remember the names of all of Liz Taylor's husbands?

TIME, SPACE, ETERNITY, AND CHANGE: Time is what he's never on. Space is what he takes up too much of in bed. An eternity is how long we could live together and he still wouldn't change.

SECURITY: Security is not a linen closet stocked with thirty tubes of toothpaste, forty boxes of Kleenex, and 120 rolls of colored toilet paper, no matter what my mother always said. Nor is security a savings account that you would rather cut your right arm off than touch, no matter what my father always said. Security is the knowledge that when you're taking a nice hot shower, and you're soapy and steamy and cozy and singing a song, your hot water positively won't run out.